More Than One Way To Be Old

by
Susan Newell

Detroit, Michigan

For AJ and Hendrix,
who I hope will someday enjoy Grandma's poems

ISBN: 979-8-218-56436-0
Cover photo: JimWest; JimWestPhoto.com

Table of Contents

Preface & Acknowledgements

I didn't begin writing poetry regularly until I was 70 — a late-blooming Boomer. Frankly, it had never occurred to me before, despite my exposure to poetry as a child and young adult.

My mother loved the poetry of the 19th and early 20th century poets. She and I would recite *Little Boy Blue* by Eugene Field, a maudlin poem about a toddler dying in his sleep. We loved it. We also loved to recite the last stanza of another death poem — *Thanatopsis*, by William Cullen Bryant. Decades passed before I could recite it without choking up.

For our lighter moods, we had *Little Orphant Annie* by James Whitcomb Riley, the so-called Hoosier poet, about a live-in servant girl who tells ghost stories to the little kids in the household right before bedtime. Each stanza ended with "An' the Gobble-uns 'at gits you Ef You Don't Watch Out!" Though we were Hoosiers ourselves, we had never heard anyone talk like Little Orphant Annie, so I assumed she was from somewhere else.

In third grade, we memorized poems and took turns reciting them to the class. The only one I remember was *In Flanders Field*, a World War I poem by Lieutenant-Colonel John McCrae, which extolled the virtue of death on the battlefield. It was an odd selection for eight-year-olds, I realized later, but then, so were *Little Boy Blue* and *Thanatopsis*. Was my later work as a hospice nurse inspired by these death poems? Perhaps.

The textbook for an introductory poetry course I took as a college freshman in 1967 contained the poems of 113 men and eight women, one of whom, Hilda Doolittle, wrote under her initials H.D. I got the message.

I did manage to write two poems when I was around 30. One mourned the death of an adopted alley cat; the other was a political rant about the implosion of a left sect I had belonged to. Both were therapeutic but took their rightful place in the dustbin of history.

For most of my adulthood, I was busy parenting, nursing, and trying to do my small part to save the world. It certainly didn't occur to me to read poetry, much less write it. After all, I had more weighty matters to attend to, and I'd already studied Keats and T.S. Eliot in college. What more was there?

After retiring at 65, my first impulse was to join several boards and committees dedicated to improving my beleaguered Detroit neighborhood. I also took on occasional short-term nursing-related jobs. My days filled up with meetings, organizing, and work.

Eventually, the stress of what began to feel like a full-time job, most of it unpaid, weighed too heavily on me, so I cut back on some of those meetings and projects. With an empty nest, parents who no longer needed my care, a lighter schedule, and more sleep, I finally freed up the bandwidth to reflect and imagine.

In 2019, another rant poem, *Upon Hearing Joe Biden's Non-Apology to Anita Hill*, came to me and demanded to be set free. Like those two poems from decades before, it landed in the dustbin, but the catharsis it provided shook something loose in my brain. I realized I had more to say and that poetry was a good way to say it.

I wouldn't have found the courage and confidence to keep writing, though, without the help of other more experienced poets. I owe special thanks to Kelly Fordon, poet and fiction writer, who leads poetry workshops through the nonprofit Springfed Arts. She created a supportive environment where I felt comfortable receiving feedback on my first clumsy efforts, and she continues to lead by kind and expert example.

Joy Gaines-Friedler was another early mentor whose repeated advice — "Show, don't tell" and "Every line a poem" — has stuck with me. She also taught me that underlining and writing in the margins is a good thing, not defacement.

Other poets in Kelly's workshops have given me thoughtful feedback and introduced me to the world of ghazals and ekphrastic poetry. I'm so grateful to Alinda Wasner, Ama Carey-Barr, Anne Doran, Brett Ashley, Ginny Grush, Linda Laderman, Marianne Peel, Mary Minock, Nancy Squires, Nancy Weatherby, and Pat Barnes. And, of course, thanks to Steve Jones, who was the first poet to see my rant poem about Biden and never said a discouraging word.

Many thanks, too, to my friend Maria Catalfio, who did the layout and cover design. With thanks and love to my husband and photographer Jim West, who took the cover photo and gave me the encouragement I needed.

Some wonderful poets I know are content to write poetry mainly for themselves. For me, writing a poem is the first step toward making a connection. It isn't complete until I've shared it with others, so I've been emailing one of my poems each month to a few dozen friends and acquaintances for the last several years. Every time I send one out, I'm making my authentic self a little better known and hopefully starting a conversation.

Now I want to pluck those poems back from cyberspace and put them in one place. Although I prefer Kindle for most of my reading, poetry demands paper. So here it is. Feel free to write in the margins.

Lament for Poems Never Written

Each day I stood before
a frosted vinyl curtain
the color of water
hanging in
the bathroom window
of my childhood home
losing myself
in a watery world
of translucent swans
swimming in the curtain
among the cattails
and lily pads
of a pond stretching
into infinity
no boundary between
water and sky
far from family
and kindergarten.

I thought of Baby Moses
bobbing gently
on the waves
in his cradle of reeds
among the bullrushes
waiting to be discovered
and start his new life.

That should have
been my first poem
but I needed a world
to give me
pencil and paper
and say
Write, little girl.

Autumn, Upstate New York

If only I could, I would swallow this day,
slather the glow of crimson and gold
over my skin, ride the shaft of sunlight
that slants just so.

I would capture these colors,
record the sound of leaves
crunched and kicked by weathered soles,
harvest the scent of leaf mold
and campfire and breeze that chills,

distill all this wonderment,
store it in a quiet corner of my soul
to take as a tonic in the days to come,
when darkness overtakes earth and sky.

Shall I Dance?

The beat, the beat, the beat
beckons me to enter
the pulse of the crowd.

My body and the beat
have long been lovers
so why are my hips now
rooted to the chair?

Once upon a time I had bad-ass hips
that could make a hula hoop dance
to my tune, up to my chest
down to my knees and back
to a tiny teenage waist.

But the hoop now betrays me
obeys only gravity
falls like an elevator
whose cable has snapped.

Still the beat, the beat, the beat
calls these old hips.
Do I dare?
Am I inspiration or fool?
And how much do I care?

I weigh my options with shoulders
swaying, with hips, these old hips
still planted in the chair.

What They Cannot Destroy

Art is not a mirror held up to reality, but a hammer
with which to shape it.   *— Bertolt Brecht*

In defiance of tyrants there will be art.
Painters will create murals that scream
with colors of fire and storm, and when
the tyrants declare them degenerate, destroy

their paints and brushes, they will paint with mud
and blood and sticks. Composers will write songs
of truth and passion, and when tyrants declare
the songs seditious, imprison those who dare sing,

music will ring from cell to cell. Poets and actors,
dancers and acrobats, comics and florists, magicians
and jugglers will flood the world with delight. Even
the spider whose web they tear will reweave again until

the tyrants surrender to a fierce, indomitable beauty.

Once Upon a Time We Were Brave

The wooden porch swing
is sturdy, wide enough
for three small girls. It hangs
from chain links the size of my fist.

The swing creaks in protest
as we test its limits. But test it
we must, for we are on a mission.

We are driving a stagecoach fleeing
bandits determined to keep us from
delivering my yellow bathing cap, I mean
gold bullion, to Fort Knox.

We pump our legs and the stagecoach
flies — over the side of the porch, over
lilies-of-the-valley sheltering in
shade on the side of the house.
Our ponytails fly.

Not once does my mother come out
to say *Stop it! You'll break your necks!*
These are the days before parents
worry about such things.

As we approach Fort Knox,
leaving the would-be robbers
dejected, dusty in the road
behind us, their horses snorting,
slathered with foam, we fly off
the swing together with a triumphant *yee-ha,*
our bodies tracing an arc in the air,
weightless in flight just before
we nail the landing.

After the pandemic

we will lean into hugs
as bittersweet as dark chocolate.

After the pandemic
six feet will be someone's height,
not the measure of a minefield.

After the pandemic
joy will visit us like an old friend
we had lost touch with.

After the pandemic
we won't need another child's
rainbow drawing on the front door
telling us we can do this hard thing.

Until then, I'll gather the tiny blue
vodka bottles scattered on a nearby
vacant lot, hang them on my crabapple tree,

and tell myself they look like sapphires.

In Praise of Homegrown Talent

Uncle Ted and Aunt Maude owned a shoe store
in Marion, Indiana, made three children and music too —
guitar, mandolin, and two voices that, after 53 years,
sounded as one.

Ted and Maude weren't famous-good or first-name good.
They were church-supper-good, local-talent-show-good,
front-porch-good. Sometimes Aunt Maude forgot a few
lyrics and had to get creative. Or Uncle Ted put the capo
on the wrong guitar fret and had to stop, move the capo,
start over in the right key. He'd shrug, make a joke,
let us know a mistake didn't matter.

I wish you could have been there the night they performed
at the Marion County Fair, 1962 it was — or maybe '63.
The stars were aligned, the air balmy, cicadas happy.
The year had been hard, but the beer went down easy.

That night Ted knew exactly where the capo went
and Maude remembered every word.
Lord, how they worked that crowd.

Their opening number was a rendition of
Keep on the Sunny Side that would have made
the Carter Family proud. If ever a song could
spread sunshine over a dark night, that was it.

With *Tennessee Waltz* we all swayed as one.
Little kids grabbed each other, twirling dancing
until they were falling down dizzy laughing.

Shenandoah, sung a capella, its harmony staying
close as new lovers, filled me with such sweet longing
I wanted to save that song in a velvet-lined box.

We all sang the chorus of *This Land is Your Land*.
Some clapped on the downbeat, some on the offbeat,
but it worked, nevertheless. One old guy sporting grizzled
salt-and-pepper beard pulled a pair of spoons from
his back pocket to tap out a galloping rhythm on his knee.

After an hour of holding us in exquisite captivity,
Ted and Maude's encore was a gentle *Amazing Grace* —
two clear voices locked tight. We closed our eyes,
all the better to hear it. And one by one we added
harmonies until that hymn had more layers
and more richness than a wedding cake.
How sweet the sound to carry us home.

What's in a Name

*On June 6, 2024, pundits were ecstatic as Detroit threw itself
a party to celebrate the rebirth of the iconic Michigan Central
Station. It had been vacant for almost four decades,
an international symbol of Detroit's decline.*

To those who called us
Murder City
who dissed us
and dismissed us
shook their heads
and tut-tutted over us
and pleasured themselves
with ruin porn

To those who declare us
Comeback City
now that the train station
is fancy as a foxy lady
heading to the club
in silver pumps

Stop telling us what we are.

We know we're a city that can
lacerate your spirit one day
and stitch it up the next

where candy wrappers and
dandelions grow in gutters
and kids hurl Kentucky-Fried
chicken bones and crumpled
napkins out the car window

where the regulars at Bert's
come on Thursday nights
to worship in the temple of jazz
and welcome all who enter
and make you giddy glad
to be alive right here right now
and forget all about chicken bones

where a neighbor with day-old
beard and leaning a little to one side
pushes his lawn mower
for the hundredth time
over the orphaned yard next door
that belongs to an investor
in a suit in Arizona
who has never met us
and doesn't wish to

where neighbors clean up a pocket park
on a summer Saturday then stick around
for hot dogs and hustle
and not a single soul feels the need
to pack heat.

For Michael

1.
1973, amidst oil crisis and recession,
I see a sad-eyed man with a cardboard sign:

Will Work For Food.
I scramble for my wallet, cursing capitalism.

But soon the jading begins. Flimsy
cardboard signs appear everywhere,

likely made from scraps on the ground,
in scrawling letters, held close to the chest

by desperate men, a few women.
Homeless Vet. Hungry. Please Help.

I begin to resent having only
a few seconds to be judge and jury.

Is he worthy? Employable? Strung out?
Quick now, what's your verdict?

I dither, let my mood and the proximity
of a dollar bill make my decision.

I hope the light will stay green
just long enough to let me pass by.

2.
A long grapevine has tethered me
to the old neighborhood for decades.

A few months ago, a friend tells me
she saw our former roommate, holding a sign.

In '73 Michael was 16 years old,
left arm scarred and withered

from a gunshot wound. Whip-smart
and gentle, wise beyond his years.

Last I heard, Michael was doing okay,
parking cars at Sindbad's.

My friend says she scolded him
at the light and gave him a twenty.

Now I keep an envelope in the side
pocket of my car, close at hand.

Zipline

If you're afraid of heights, do it. If you're terrified, don't. Advice from the Costa Rican tour guide, taken to heart. She may be afraid, but she's plucky. She will do it.

Standing on the wooden platform encased in heavy harness, blood red helmet, floppy leather gloves, holding the round metal gizmo that the handsome guide will hook to the zipline, she wonders if she has overestimated her courage. Her stomach is knotted in protest, her breathing shallow. Straight ahead is only sky and treetops. Looking down not an option.

She had imagined herself sitting upright, like a skier enjoying the view from a chairlift, only faster. But no, she is told to lean way back, straighten her arms, bend and lift her knees, cross her ankles, assume the frightened posture of an omega dog confronted by the alpha.

If this is a mistake, she must live or die with it, as her only option now is the plunge. As she is launched into the abyss, she hears the full-throated scream of someone trapped in the melding of ecstasy and terror.
It's her scream.

She sails in a cocoon of gale-force wind and the high-pitched metal zinging of gizmo sliding along zipline. The gizmo has handles that she will use to brake, but only if she feels the zipline sway from side to side, a signal from the landing crew. In her fear-addled mind, loosening her grip on the handles means certain death, so she keeps them in a stranglehold with aching hands.

Don't waste this moment, she tells herself, relaxing just enough to open her eyes and look beyond the treetops to mountains sloping gently to the ocean in a glorious blur. A bit of scarlet glances off the corner of her vision, as she and a macaw share the kinship of flight.

Already she must prepare to land, but she is still going so fast — much too fast. She didn't feel the signal to brake, but can she be sure? So much happening at once, she has been distracted, perhaps she missed it. Taking control, she toggles the handles back and forth, frantic and still flying. She is close enough now to see the excited faces of the guide and other zipliners waiting on the platform. Do they not see disaster coming in 5, 4, 3....?

In last-second surrender, our plucky septuagenarian takes the proper stance for landing, straightening her legs, feet wide, bracing for a warp-speed ending.

Bedtime Ritual

The curves of my father's back
are familiar as I slowly walk
the length of his spine, carefully
realigning vertebrae one by one.

He oofs with each step but says
not to worry, it's a good hurt.
After all, how much damage
can a 5-year-old do?

After my chiropractic treatment
I lie down to hear *The Moose,*
The Mouse, and the Louse,
a tale he created just for me.

In each telling, he makes the same
mistake. Each time I say *No Daddy,*
the mouse was sitting on the moose's
ear, not the other way around!
Oh that's right! he says. We laugh.

In the early evening, my father
is a stern-eyed stranger lost
in a book by some scientist
or theologian. I know better
than to speak to strangers.

But for these few minutes
each night we are good
buddies, lying side by side
in the dark, sharing a joke.

Dorothy's Hands

My mother's hands were plain but rich
with veins like roads on a map leading
somewhere important. Between the veins,
shallow valleys a child could daydream in.
Sensible nails filed just above the quick,
like a sliver of new moon.

I see the hands of a pioneer, ready to
knead bread dough at daybreak or
wring a chicken's neck for dinner.

Dorothy never made bread
from scratch or killed a chicken
as far as I know, but her hands
were ready.

Hers were the hands that apprenticed
me in the art of making pie crust.
Hands cool and comforting when
my forehead felt feverish, annoying
when they stroked my ravaged
adolescent face, pushed bangs
from my eyes.

She told me how beautiful
my own hands were —
a landscape without roads
or valleys, fingers long and slender,
half-moon nails perfectly oval —
the hands of a pianist she said.

Now I clip my nails into new moons,
study my hand's veined map.
Dorothy had such beautiful hands.
Another thing I neglected to tell her.

Williamsburg, Iowa, July 2020

Our motel rises from
a freshly-mown hill above
elegant cornfields, where
green tassels brush a little below
the elephant's eye.
Evening sun slants just so
on hills rolling to infinity
in shades of emerald and lime.

It's corn weather,
the air a physical presence,
hot and strong enough to carry
the heavy chatter of a million cicadas.

Interstate-80 below
will carry us back soon
to the land of veils and troubled souls.
In this hot, green, and heavy world,
no need to think of masks,
yet I do. Always and everywhere.

A fellow traveler lounges outside his room,
his face weathered and nearly toothless,
shocking yellow t-shirt, ample belly,
baseball cap hiding the flow of white
pandemic-length hair.

From nothing more than this,
I create a story of otherness,
wonder if he is a good friend of
Jim Beam and the president.

We recite the script of fellow travelers,
where we're going,

what route we're taking.
is corn weather too hot, or just right?

These days no one escapes talk
of that other world for long.
Turns out we have the same view
of our bitter reality.
We lapse into easy silence,
listening to the cicadas
while I edit my story.

The Art & Lessons of Pie Crust

At eight, I declare myself our family's pie
crust maker. Like apprentices of old,
I have learned the art at my mother's elbow.

The task begins sensuously, my fingers
massaging the silky softness of flour, salt,
and Crisco. I could linger here forever

but if there is to be pie I must add water now
which I dread. The creaminess of flour
and fat turns into sticky clumps

which I scrape off my fingers in disgust.
Quickly I press the mixture into a ball.
Now comes the call for courage and optimism.

I sprinkle flour on the table, spread it
to make a landing pad for the dough.
Let boys have their beloved baseball bats,

I have my grandmother's wooden rolling pin.
Pressing it deep into the dough, I begin
the rhythmic rolling, turning, pressing outward

dusting with flour as needed.
The rolling pin makes a soft and satisfying
clunk with each stroke. If the pie gods

are content, this step will be a meditation
on the zen of pie making. But these are fickle
gods, known to take pleasure in torturing

small children. Too often the dough sticks,
tears, fans out at odd angles defying
the shape of any pie pan. At least once

I must return this misshapen disk to a ball,
resist the urge to throw it across the room,
and start the rhythmic rolling again.

In the battle of wills between me
and the pie gods I prevail, coaxing the thin
full moon of dough into the pan,

patching holes, prodding dough into place.
At last my thumbs take a victory lap around
the pan's perimeter, fluting its edges into waves.

Give a child flour, fat, salt, water
and the promise of pie, and in this alchemy
she will learn all she needs to know of grit.

Old Love

How could I have known then,
watching an old couple in the diner
staring at coffee — I assumed, into mugs
of regret, gazing past each other,
the well of conversation long run dry,

how could I have known then,
blinded by pity and youth, vowing
never to settle for less than a bottomless
well of words — nights filled with pillow
talk, news of the day, philosophies of life,

how could I have known then,
that our own silences would grow lush
with memory — a disastrous honeymoon
transformed into a story told again
and again, an endless flow of endearingly
bad jokes, times when love went missing
then came home to feasting, petty sharp
grievances dulled by age, times we clung
to each other in wild winds,

how could I have known then
that memory and presence and a cup
of coffee shared in easy silence
would so often be enough?

Raining on the White Folks' Picnic

We gather on a clear day, neighbors
sharing burgers, potato salad,
and assumptions about the world.
We have blessings to count,
a softball game to play.

A single cloud drops
a name, Michael Brown,
a whisper on a neighbor's arm.
Did you feel something?
Not really, says another.

Then another drop, another name.
Tamir Rice.
Yes, I feel it, just a sprinkle though,
not enough to stop the game.

At first we count the names
of the slain as they fall,
note each one landing,
say the name aloud.
Freddie Gray.
Alton Sterling.

Soon there are too many to count,
too many to say, much less recall.

The sky opens in a torrent
battering us, ruining the game,
creating little pools of the dead
at first base. Heads down, we run
to take shelter because we
are the lucky ones who can hide,
huddling together
to allay the sudden chill,
praying we won't drown.

After the Basement Flood

Fragments of my youth are heading to a landfill today.
First grade report card — *Susan is a pleasure to have in class* —
made the trip with a 4th grade report on honeybees,
my first lesson in the power of community.
A few letters from college better off buried.

I'm surprised to feel no deep sense of loss,
just a vague dis-ease. Truth be told,
I'd forgotten the contents of those boxes,
but the idea of them was comforting.

I'd imagined them providing hours
of entertainment in my dotage,
something to chuckle over in my wheelchair,
sparking a flood of memories from which
to write my memoirs,
surely of great interest to many.

What's left now is faulty memory
which like a house painter's brush
re-creates my history in broad strokes
and bold colors, no longer limited
by artifacts to keep me tethered to the facts.
Only beholden now to fragments of truth.

Christina Tells the Backstory

After *Christina's World* by Andrew Wyeth

Andy says I remind him of a crab, dragging myself around
our farm, and I'm okay with that. Crabs get where they
need to go. These skinny arms serve me well enough to
bring me to the field each day just to feel small under
endless sky, to study the horizon, and have a chat with
Eternity. Also to see how the new roof looks from a
distance. I just wish Alvaro would put the damned ladder
back where it belongs.

Andy's painting gives me a dreamy feeling, like looking at
the stained glass window in church or soaking in a warm
bath. But that's not me on the ground — not exactly. The
head and torso are Betsy, his much younger wife. I was his
muse, Andy says, not his model. Guess I can't blame him
for liking her body better than mine. You lose a shade of
truth when you tell someone else's story, but I guess that's
just how art works.

You should know I'm not stranded out there. I just like
moving low, feeling the prickly grass, inspecting the wild
white clover and ants as I go. I know ants in ways you
high-riders never will.

And when I get back to this old house that I love like my
own soul, these gnarled hands will make a perfect cup to
catch a drink of cool water from the pump.

Tchaikovsky Reacts to Ellington & Strayhorn

On September 19, 1960, Columbia Records released Duke
Ellington and Billy Strayhorn's The Nutcracker Suite,
a reimagining of Tchaikovsky's ballet score.

Boxhe moy, my God, what have you done
to my work — no, my child! who danced so gaily, lightly
with fairest wings of strings and woodwinds.
But you, with your vulgar brass, rhythm slanted, drunken!
I could not listen beyond the first notes.

And yet…and yet after a night of fitful sleep, my dreams
haunted by lazy trombones, I was compelled to return
for reasons I can't yet divine.

Where I brought order, you create chaos, so many voices —
brass, always the brass pushing my strings almost
into the wings. And saxophone slip-sliding over the scales.
A dance without structure, save the syncopation of drums.

Such music is not chaste — indeed creates (dare I say it?)
a sensual mood, invitation to move shoulders and hips,
to rise to the dance floor and move with wild abandon.
Perhaps, I admit, a tonic for bitter Russian winters….

I have listened countless times now, and though I do not
approve, though I do not believe your suite suitable for
the delicate ears of women and children, I am intrigued by
your unorthodox approach, wondering what you might
have made of *Sleeping Beauty*.

Now that I'm invisible

perhaps I'll do something audacious.
Now that the white of my hair
renders others blind, perhaps
I'll rob a bank.

I can hear the young teller,
trying to describe me to the police.
She looked kind of, you know,
....old.

If they caught me, I needn't fear
the lineup with five other old women.
We'd stand there in our decrepitude,
thinning hair, sagging chins, fighting
the urge to smile to make ourselves
seem more pleasant.

The nice young teller would be stumped.

Now that I'm invisible, there's a lightness
in my step as I walk past groups
of young men. No need to suck in
my stomach, straighten my posture,
feeling their sharp gaze cut through me.

My cohorts speak of getting older.
Older than what? When will we be old?
Let them curse the heartless Universe
while I shake off regret and head to the bank.

Greetings From the Pleistocene

Long before visitors to Yosemite
began striking playful Instagram
poses among the giant sequoias,

and long before a graffiti artist
began spraying *GASM*
around downtown Detroit,

and long before my big brother
carved his initials in wet cement
on our sidewalk,

and long before American GIs
scrawled *Kilroy was here*
on walls in France and the South Pacific,

and long before ancient Puebloan children
stenciled their hands with red ochre
on dusty boulders in the Utah desert,

beetle-browed hominin children
of the windy Tibetan Plateau,
not yet walking fully upright,

pressed their hands and feet
into soft travertine limestone,
marking their place in the world.

The Unbearable Reality of Fluorescence
After Edward Hopper's *Nighthawks*

His thought bubble:

funny what lighting can do for a dame ... she looked so
luscious in the darkness at the bar ... hair glowing red as a
fox in the candlelight ... pressed her lips to the cigarette I
offered ... held my hand to steady it as I flicked the lighter
... turned her head and blew a slow trail of smoke off to
the side through full red lips, like in the movies ... the wife
couldn't do that with a cigarette if you gave her a million
bucks ... the 40-watt hotel room light held the mood ... but
damn these diner lights! they kill the magic...show you
everything you don't wanna see ... silver strands spoiling
the bottle-red hair ... mascara smudged under eyes with
crows' feet fit for a grandma .... how many times you
gonna be a chump Joe?

Her thought bubble:

why'd we decide to come here for coffee anyway? ....
he seemed so sweet in the bar ... shoulda left it at that
... pretty sure he said his name was Joe ... made me feel
special again ... like Fred used to ... but at the hotel?...
no foreplay no afterglow none of that ... this guy made
Fred look like Casanova in bed ... and what the hell
kinda dumbbell tells a girl he's single when the tan line
on his ring finger tells the truth ... too bad they invented
fluorescent lights ....think I'll make a pot roast when
Fred comes back .... Fred loves pot roast.

Oak Tree vs. 21st Century

Men from DTE came to trim our tree today,
a century-old oak canopy over the backyard.

When I think to look up now and then
into its lush overstory
I see my own version of god's face.

This oak allows my shade-loving
plants to grow at its feet,
makes a playscape for squirrels
to chase each other like feral children,
acorns for them to toss on our heads,
for my husband to collect in a jar on his desk.

But the branches threaten power lines
so must be hacked off by men
just doing their jobs,
tossing chunks of history onto my hostas,
choosing by rules known only to tree
trimmers and their bosses,
what Nature gets to stay,
what must go.

This Old Garage

Our next door neighbor's garage
has been devolving for decades.
Its southern wall hugs our giant hostas.
Right angles have disappeared.
It leans like a boxer beaten bloody,
still clinging to the ropes.

The roof has morphed into wide
swaths of sky, welcoming
chickadees, squirrels, and possibly
creatures I don't wish to know.

Our neighbors have wanted
to take it down for years,
but extra cash eludes them,
so time and weather must do
the work of men and machines.

From my Adirondack chair
on summer days, I can almost see
a decaying barn on an abandoned
farm in Iowa, hear the ghosts of cows
mooing, a tractor humming in the distance.

My bucolic retreat in a city
where we all make do.

To the Mothers of Tyre's Killers, From Another Mother

On January 7, 2023, Tyre Nichols, a young Black man, was
severely beaten by five Black Memphis police officers.
He died of his injuries three days later.

Surely you must have given your own boy
The Talk, told him exactly what to say and do,
what not to say, what not to do. All that worry
now turned inside out upside down.

Have you seen the video, picked out
your baby from the tangle
of arms and legs, batons and boots,
just like you picked him out
in the nursery among rows of sacred
bundles, swaddled and laid
in their plastic mangers?

Do you ask yourself how this could be
the same boy who knew to say please
and thank you, learned to sit still in church,
helped his grandma carry in the groceries?

Can this be the same little boy who asked
for one more story, a drink of water,
and to please please scare away
the monster in his closet?

Is this the same young man who walked
across the stage, flipped his tassel,
gave you that little lopsided smile
when he spotted you in the crowd?

Do you wonder how your boy,
so proud and handsome in his
new uniform could morph into
a dead-eyed mug shot?

Do you weep in the night, ask
God how you can carry the weight
of such heavy love?
Do you ask Him to please please
unravel time, take back the night
when your baby forgot who raised him
and turned you into collateral damage?

It's Party Central in My Aging Brain

The party's in full swing
in the cramped apartment
in my head. Random Thoughts
gather in the tiny kitchen, jostle,
excuse themselves and move on.

Brilliant Idea holds forth, but is cut
short as her audience drifts away
to a more interesting conversation.

Great Plan calls for everyone's
attention, but the music is loud,
and the din created by
Random Thoughts and Brilliant Idea
makes Great Plan feel irrelevant.

Poetry muscles her way to the center
of the room and demands to be
heard. Train of Thought,
poor thing, keeps getting lost
on her way to the bathroom.

As the host of this chaos, I must
make room for them all but do wish
they could be more orderly.
I settle in a corner and wait for
Acceptance to bring me a margarita.

Two at the Ladder

We take our places
for an annual late autumn
ritual — my husband at the top
of the ladder, me at the bottom
holding it steady. A year of nature
has gathered in the gutters and must
be tossed to the ground. I have finally
learned to wear a hat. I will say that this
is absolutely the last year I will allow him
to take such a risk. He is too old to be on tall
ladders, I say. Next year, I will hire someone
younger, more agile to clean gutters — someone
who will not ask me to hold his life in my hands.
I have said this each year and mean it. He will assure
me that someday he may be too old. He will let me know
when that time comes. He's sorry, he says, for taking so long,
tossing so much dirt on my head. I don't mind. I'm writing a
poem.

Yes, I know there is much to do

but bear with me today, for I must turn away
turn away and choose instead to nap and dream
I am flying on gossamer wings to Xanadu.

Bear with me. After my nap today I will
eat a bowl of whipped cream as big as my head
with my grandmother's silver soup spoon.

Bear with me now, as I submerge myself
in a tub of bubbles and read a novel of love
and passion in some utopian land far away.

Bear with me, as I paint each toenail
a different shade of blue while listening to
Yo-Yo Ma and imagine taking up the cello.

Bear with me today, when I dance on blue-
toed bare feet to the driving beat of
Do You Wanna Dance? Yes, yes I do.

Bear with me.
I do feel the pull of gravity and dread
but today I choose delight instead.

Soup Line, March 2020

I come each morning
for my daily ration of news.
I must know. I cannot bear it.
Its bitterness bites my tongue,
roils my stomach,
yet I devour it
like a starving person
reduced to eating grass.

Some days I skip
the soup line,
but always I return.
I cannot eat.
I must eat.

Two Faces of Winter

1.
Damn you Floridians,
who will never know the cold
or the sound of scraper hacking
windshield ice in 6 a.m. darkness,

or needles inhaled with every
breath as the temperature plunges
to lows that should only be
experienced by frozen peas.

You will never forget the look
and feel of sunlight. Never know
the wet shiver of snow sliding down
your neck from a well-placed snowball.

You will never race bitter wind
to the front door, stomp snowy boots,
and curse the pain
of dead toes being resurrected.

You will never need fleece,
but will stretch out barefoot
on your lounge chair,
sip pina coladas,
plan to play nine holes tomorrow.

Perhaps a bit of cognac with Miles Davis
will ease my pain, soothe me into
a northern kind of warm.

2.
Poor Floridians, you will never know
the crunch and squeak of boots
on packed snow, the tickle and crackle
in your nose as you see with every
exhalation what being alive looks like.

You will never fall dramatically
into snow angel pose,
build a snow fort, or feel
the satisfying splat of a snowball
hitting its mark, never know
the delicious anticipation
of the cold white revenge to come.

You will never lose yourself in winter blue
sky pure and exhilarating as new love.

You will never feel the rush
of warm air that makes cheeks
and toes tingle as they come alive.

You will never light candles and feel
the luxury of fleece on bare feet
as you fold yourself into the couch,
cradle a steaming mug of ginger tea,
believe in and breathe in its healing powers,

and let the cool jazz of Miles Davis
steep you in a northern kind of warm.

Reframe as Needed

My
second
favorite scar
is buried now
in the wrinkles
of my hand, remnant
of the time I sharpened
a chef's knife with glorious
exuberance, lifting it above
my head and bringing it down
into the groove of the sharpener
over and over, channeling Leonard
Bernstein thrusting his baton onto the
podium for the last dramatic notes of
Beethoven's Fifth, his face glistening
with sweat, his hair a hot mess of passion.
But this performance ended on my thumb,
not a C-major chord, and I paid for it in
blood and six stitches. We use cocoa butter
and other potions to erase our scars and
memories of the carelessness or hubris
or simple misfortune that created them.
    But I miss my
    scar, souvenir
    of the one and
    only time I
    conducted
    the New York
    Philharmonic.

A Meditation on Chairs

Two Adirondack chairs rest beyond our window
under three inches of snow, angled toward
each other as though having a conversation.

Yet they remain silent, perhaps too cold and forlorn
to speak. We could have given them shelter months
ago, far from winter's assault, but we are lazy

and have no good winter home for them anyway.
We are shortening their lives, as we have other chairs
before them. I tell myself I like the weathered look,

but if I took the time to interrogate my obligation
to cheap wood, which I don't, perhaps I'd have
to admit that's just an excuse. These chairs

have served us well, held us for conversations over
the years, some as weighty as the state of the world,
others light and easy as what to have for dinner. I love

how they let my body sink into an angle suitable for repose,
even lethargy. From here I can look up into the leafy
canopy and wonder why I don't sit here more often

to consider the nature of Nature, of oaks and sparrows,
but we lacked foresight in building this patio,
not knowing that in summer each late afternoon sun

would find a way to evade the shade and bear down
upon our heads. These chairs don't know or care
that late afternoon is my preferred time to do nothing.

I deserve better, and so do these chairs, I suppose.

Groceries on the Go

Miles to go before we sleep,
we stop in Middle of Somewhere, Iowa.

In my husband's world, grocery shopping
has all the appeal of an oil change.

Beating his personal best — seven minutes
door to door — requires us to divide and conquer.

He takes cheese, crackers, soup, cereal.
My mission: bananas, bread, milk.

The aisle to bananas is lined with snowy
hydrangeas, calling for a light caress

and a moment of reflection on the nature of Beauty.
Jars of red pepper bruschetta and marinated feta

lure me to a nearby shelf, promising to marry happily
on a bed of Triscuits. Soft mist from the lettuce

sprayer bathes me as I circle past Romaine
and Bibb, back to bananas, marveling

at how many shades of green co-exist in Nature.
Rutabaga, that pale homely rock, lies next

to spring mix, as if in defiance.
Why does rutabaga even exist?

If I ever write a poem about orphan veggies,
they will certainly be root....

Are we done? He peers into my empty cart.
I ignore the familiar clench of his jaw,

see that yet again he has bought store-brand
tomato soup not Campbell's, Ritz not Triscuits.

Twelve minutes later, we are heading west
on I-80. He considers our next rest stop

and surfs radio stations. I consider cornfields
and the many meanings of forbearance.

Abandoned Coal Mine, Beckley, WV

He speaks as though conscious
of his next breath, the lilt
of West Virginia mountains in his voice.

Coal's in my blood. Where else would I work?
At the end of the day, I'm proud I supported
my family,

After 35 years coal is in Jack's lungs too.
He scrambles on the hamster wheel
of bureaucracy, fights indifferent men
in white coats and suits.
.
Coal took its toll on his back too. Now his job
is to bring this dead mine back to life
for those who cannot imagine life
in such a dark place - drilling holes, packing
explosives, lighting fuses, getting the hell out.

Three hundred feet below sunlight now, Jack says
working 1,000 feet down is better. Coal seams wider,
no need to slide yourself into a space as tight
as a slave ship.

A visitor from around here recalls the disaster
at Upper Big Branch in 2010, 29 miners choked
on methane, coal dust, and corporate money.

Bill told me something bad would happen.
Just a matter of time. Company, government,
didn't do their jobs. And you know what?
CEO got a year in prison — on a golf course.

Jack and the visitors share a litany of the dead —
Jason Atkins
Bill Lynch
Joe Marcum ...

I knew a lot of 'em. All of 'em my brothers.

Jack takes a long breath, shakes his head,
continues the tour.

I'm No Colin Kaepernick

I sit in the stands near third base, waiting for my only
Tigers game of the season, for my chance to fulfill a pledge
never to sing or stand for the national anthem again.

I'm surprised by the fluttering in my stomach. This can't
be as hard as the few times I've been hauled away by cops.

I felt exhilarated then, riding a wave of solidarity and
righteousness, buoyed by the crowd and by youth.
Today I feel alone, just me and my principles.

Taking a knee isn't easy at my age, in a tight space, on
concrete no less. It feels silly, performative. I'll settle for
staying seated and silent — defiant but not in pain.

The stakes for me are very low. It won't change the course
of my life as it did his. Won't destroy my career.
Granted, he landed softly on a $20 million bed. But still...

How must it feel to face down the hatred of self-proclaimed
patriots calling you a traitor?
Granted, he's found new purpose, perhaps an even greater
calling. But still...

Did he know the price he'd pay? He must have suspected
that the power of one Black man who plays the game is no
match for those who own it and think they own his voice.

The truth is, I never liked the song. Most folks need a step
ladder to reach the high notes.
The truth is, by the time we get to *O'er the land of the free*,
I'm exhausted.

Will I be challenged, harassed by the zealous fans around me? I doubt it.
Being an old white woman does have its perks. But still...

The music begins, the announcer tells us to stand, and all those around me obey.
Men take off their caps. I close my eyes, bow my head, and pretend to pray.

To George Floyd's Murderer

It's so much easier this way,
isn't it officer?
No need to find a rope
a stool
a tree.
No need to buy gasoline
to burn the body afterwards.
That was so 20th century.
Now all you need is handcuffs
a state-issued badge
a steady knee
and the weight of 400 years
on a Black man's neck.

To the One Who Stood Guard
as George Floyd was murdered

Your face carries
a familiar blankness:
elevator-face,
standing-in-line face,
waiting-for-bus face,
don't-give-a-damn face.

And those eyes,
so empty, unseeing,
like you're trapped
in the dark recesses of a cave,
eyes only useful now as an
escape route for your soul.

Your ears must be filled
with some light-hearted tune
you heard on the radio
as you put on your badge
and came to work today.
Surely the volume in your head
is turned up so loud
that you can't hear the cries,

or the long silence that follows.

Vacant Parking Lot Vendor

I never did stop to try those ribs
from a man standing over smoky grill
in sun and drizzle. His confident moves
as he flipped the sizzling meat
suggested the ribs might be worth a try.

Each day I drove by but had no time,
not today, perhaps tomorrow.
Each day I told myself a story
of resilience, a man in survival mode
making the best of what he had.
Perhaps if I stopped,
I would confirm the story,
or lay it to rest.

Perhaps if I stopped, I would make a new
acquaintance — someone to greet by name.
Perhaps if I stopped, I would taste ribs so rich,
so falling-off-the-bone tender
they would make me hum.

Today in place of this guy, that grill, those ribs,
weeds pushing through cracked asphalt capture
Skittles and Swishers wrappers from dry wind.

Rumination

A conversation with you
stuck in my head at two
in the morning is a road
with no destination.

On a circular track
I keep coming back
to what you did and said
what I felt and meant
in an endless loop
of recrimination.

I play the words back
again and again
saying each time
more clearly
compellingly
telling you kindly
how you were wrong
and how we can
make it right.

At three I see
sleep deprivation's
my fate,
at least for tonight.

After dozing and dreaming
nonsensical claims
and retorts
I arise in first light
ready to talk,
hoping for sweet
vindication.

Trash Talking the Flimflam Wall Street Man

I pity the man (let's call
him Stan) who dares to insist
privilege doesn't exist.

He denies the prize
he received when his eyes
first opened to find
he'd been born in a cradle
of love pure white,
with a mouthful of silver
on a blanket of clover.

Stan beams with pride
as he rides on a rainbow,
a smooth glide to the gold
he can spend
from the pot at the end.

Stan supposes the bed
of roses he lies in bloomed
in the warmth of his charm.

He never thinks to thank
parents who nurtured his nature,
ensured he always got more than
his share of toys and tutors
and suitable suitors.

He tries to deny that the big piece
of pie he's been served
with a side dish of equity —
the private kind that he won't
need to share — is related at all
to his ocean-side view at the top

of the cliff, at the head of the stair.
No, says Stan, smarts and hard work
got me there.

Oh Stan, you're not the man
you thought you were,
you arrogant twit!

More Than One Way To Be Old

Why be one who longs to see
the Northern Lights once more,
promises to go just as soon as
the dishes are done
the house clean
the leaves raked
and the stars correctly aligned?

Let me glance at the clock to see
time has reached warp speed,
arise from the table heedless
of dishes in the sink
leaves asunder
heedless of the location of stars,
to seek that place where
the night sky flickers
emerald and violet.

Gender Gap

Never ask a young guy stocking shelves
at CVS where to find bath powder puffs.
He will give you a blank stare.

As you try to describe the obvious
he will ask a buddy,
who will also look befuddled.

You will wonder if English is no longer
the lingua franca here but you will persist.

Perhaps they think you are speaking
of some mid-20th century artifact
like a garter belt or a landline.

Once the CVS guys understand
it's a device for applying bath powder
they will show you a round bath sponge.

You will shake your head, but the CVS guys
will have lost interest by now.
They don't need, and indeed
have never needed, powder puffs.

You will go home and tell
your husband this story.
He will give you a blank stare.

Open Mic Night at Bert's

The darkness carries static energy
and the faint scent of beer and barbecue
as we slide into our wobbly wooden chairs
at tables set up as close as our next breath.

The chaos of a crowded bar
bounces off hot pink and lavender walls.
The black and white checkerboard
floor is enough to make you feel
dizzy even before your first drink.

In this community of jazz,
those who create it mingle
easily with those of us who just
need it. Folks improvise a dance
to avoid collisions around the bar,
but still, sometimes strangers
bump into each other.
Everyone laughs, says *Excuse me,*
exchanges knowing smiles.

The show begins a little late
but we don't care. The good times
have started to roll even before
the first singer steps to the stage.

Everyone who signed up will get
their moment in the spotlight
of the SBH Jazz Trio — keyboard,
drums, and upright bass.
They'll follow you anywhere
on the scale in any key, carry you
if you falter, make you sound like
music should be your day job.

Lady Day is one of the regulars.
With a gardenia behind one ear,
her dreamy eyes, voice languid and sandy
as a drummer's brushes slowly drawing
circles on a snare drum tell us
Billie Holliday's in the house.

The trio starts up a James Carter
composition and from a crowded table,
the man himself appears, just home
from a European tour. He threads his way
to the stage and commands his sax
to sing, dance, and finally let out
a long primal scream.

Somehow James knows just how far
he can push his instrument,
how far he can push the audience.
Just at the point where pleasure
meets pain, he fades out, acknowledges
the shouts and applause with a smile and nod,
and lets another musician feel the love.

William, who seems like he's always
been on the wrong side of hard times,
gets up next to share his story — a halting
blues he's composing on the spot.

And the next day at court…
the judge says to me…

We applaud politely each time he pauses,
thinking he's finished, but no, he's just
trying to recall what the judge said next.

Eventually we begin to laugh and cheer
each time he launches into the next verse
until finally the mic is gently removed
from William's hand, and he bows deeply
to our standing ovation.

Apollo's Chariot

The roar of motorcycle engines
crashes through our quiet conversation
on the patio of a hip restaurant.
We shake our heads.
These young people.

As the parade rolls by, one rider
rises from his seat, stands proud as
the figurehead on a tall ship,
one leg thrust back like the tailfin
of a '59 Cadillac Eldorado,
his black helmet streaked
with flames, feeling the power
of facing down the wind,
so alive, so lucky to be young.

Do-Over

I loved the scratch-scratch
of my grandmother's butter knife
scraping burnt toast, sweeping
flakes of char into the sink
like a skift of black snow.

Grandma never got the toaster setting right,
never recognized the acrid smell
of bread burning until it was too late.

But no matter. She'd scrape-scrape,
Good as new, and place
the dry resurrected toast
on a pale green Melmac plate
next to her daily breakfast
of hot water and stewed prunes.

First Memory

Blinded by the spotlight,
wrapped in the warmth of darkness,

I'm honored to be representing
this great country

at nursery school graduation.
My crown and torch of gold paper

give me more gravitas
than any 4-year-old should expect.

I may be shy, but give me
God Bless America,

and I can sing it over the heads
of parents, to the rooftops and beyond,

my voice strong and clear
as mountain water.

The butterflies inside me say
They love you. All is well.

I am content, knowing this feeling
will last forever.

Seeking Respite, July 2020

Let us go at dusk into the woods
to find our perfect marshmallow sticks,
while one of us stays to build a fire,
positioning twigs just so,
adding paper to create a hungry blaze.

Let's sit together on separate logs,
carefully spaced,
to watch the fire
and bring out old songs
from the rusty file drawer
of our youth.
We'll help each other
remember the words
and laugh when we all forget.

As the fire dies down
we'll seek out small
pockets of embers
and debate the proper way
to toast a marshmallow
as we twirl our sticks.
What comfort we'll find
in arguments over things
of no consequence!

When our fingers are white
and sticky, and we are full
of happy guilt for eating
one s'more too many,
we'll let the conversation
die down with the flames
and let the embers warm
our faces, and lull us into

sweet mindless reverie,
heedless of the cold
and threatening darkness
at our backs.

Calling Time Out

Today I must think of small things.
I am weary, and the big things
too terrifying to consider.
We once declared another world
possible but did not expect this.

Like Sisyphus we pushed
and pushed the boulder,
but gravity was too strong,
our muscles too weak,
even when we moved in synchrony.

I cannot bear the weight
of the world now but can still
move small stones.
Today, seeking respite
even from pebbles

I'll finish my coffee
as woodpeckers and chickadees
jostle each other for suet
outside my kitchen window,
then armed with litter grabber,

rid my block of candy wrappers,
cigarette butts, and other small things
weighing down this too heavy world.

This is Just to Say

With apologies to William Carlos Williams,
who wrote a poem by the same name.

I have taken
the tires
that were on
your Ford Focus

and which
you were probably
needing
to get to work today

Forgive me
they were perfect
so new
and so round

Another Reason I Haven't Hired a House Cleaner

We sit at the kitchen table — Mother,
Mattie and me. Mattie takes the place
reserved for Daddy at dinnertime.
My mother has laid out her specialty —
ham salad sandwiches — for our lunch.

After a morning spent bringing order
to chaos, Mattie recounts the latest
petty transgressions of her husband
Osella. She speaks in the slow cadence
of her Alabama home. Mother loves
these stories, says *they're so
entertaining.* She says they give her
insight into how colored people live.

Mother appreciates that Mattie
is mild-mannered — not like those
Negroes whose laughter is too loud,
whose gestures too bold. Mother does
her best imitation of how she thinks
Black people laugh. Not when Mattie
is around, of course. Mother says she
admires colored people who are nice
and refined — people like Nat King Cole.
I am uneasy when my mother says this,
but I am young and don't know why.

My parents pay into Social Security
for Mattie, though they could surely
get away with paying her under
the table. It's just the right thing to do.
Mother gives Mattie a ride home after
each cleaning to save her the long bus ride.

When rage erupts in the South
of the '60s, my parents cannot
understand the white-hot hate
behind firehoses and police dogs.
Our dinner table is filled with
righteous anger toward the haters.

Mattie's visits continue into her 80s.
With her failing rheumy eyes,
arthritic knees, the cleaning devolves
into a few swipes of a dust cloth,
sandwiches, and storytelling.
Mother would never let Mattie go,
knowing how much she needs the money.

At Mattie's funeral, our family gets
a mention in the program. My mother
mourns Mattie's passing but takes
comfort in the knowledge that she has
always been good to our cleaning lady.

Years later in a stressful time
I hire a house cleaner. The first day
entering my home with every room
clean and smelling of Pledge
brings me to happy tears.
A few months later I let her go.
I'll get a house cleaner when
I'm old, I say.

Now my body tells me it's okay to put
away the broom and mop, but my
mind can't sweep away the memory
of Mattie, my mother, and me
at the kitchen table over ham salad
sandwiches, Mattie entertaining
Mother with stories of her life.

A Hospice Nurse Considers Dylan Thomas

Do not go gentle into that good night,
But rage, rage against the dying of the light.
                    Dylan Thomas

I made my living from the dying, embracing
those who raged, sitting in stillness with
ones on a gentler path, bade them all
safe travels as they left to meet
with angels and ancestors
or more likely to meld
into the great reunion
of worms.

I heard my mother rage against the dying
of the light as she cursed the toll
a century of living had taken
on her body. Her last words —
It's disgusting.

Will I rage? Perhaps, but what I hope for
is this: to explore the reflections and
refractions of the light with fierce
curiosity, to carpe every diem,
bathe each day in metaphor.

And when the light begins to dim, I will
say *How romantic is the candlelight,*
And when I have sucked the last
of life's juice and I am too
weary to seize another day

When the light is too dim to distinguish
delight from dirt, may I think
How lovely was the light,
and what a good good night.

Moment of Grace

In midriff top and short shorts
Billy leans over Michael's bed.
Their father stands tall
on the other side in the crisp
buttoned-down shirt and khakis
befitting a former Marine.

AIDS will take both brothers —
one soon, the other likely facing
a few more embattled years.
Decades of recrimination,
attack and counter-attack,
have made the air toxic
in the no-man's-land
between father and sons.

Now the air lightens
feels expansive
holding them all tenderly
as the folding in begins —

Michael's eyes sink deeper
as if all they need to see now
lies within
cheeks hollow
mouth a gentle downturn
breath shallow
its rhythm irregular as love.

As the father lays a hand
on Michael's forehead
Billy takes Michael's hand
reaches across the bed
to take their father's.

Tortilla Maker, Oaxaca, Mexico

No grass in the yard of your home,
chickens peck and scratch the dirt,
a rusty one-speed bike lying in dust
next to overturned steel washtub.

Your voice soft and confident
draws me into your story,
the lilt of Spanish alternating
with the clarity of translation.

At handmade oven of brick and fire
in bright turquoise apron, dusty huaraches,
you tell us of a local nonprofit,
a small loan, and your new life
as a businesswoman.

Your weathered hands press and toss
masa dough from hand to hand,
lay it gently on the hot comal
as one might lay a newborn down to sleep.

With fingers hardened by thousands of turns
and burns you fearlessly flip the tortilla
at just the right moment.
It comes off hot and crisp.

You offer to let us try
and one by one our doughy newborns
crumple on the comal as we laugh.

I am curious, a maker of stories.
I walk past a suburban mansion
or meet a tortilla maker in Mexico
and wish to drift like night air

into those homes, materializing
in a stranger's living room.

Would we find common ground,
if only a shared favorite color,
love for our children?

I do not know your life, Señora Francisca,
but I know this: You must be proud.
*Sus tortillas son las más deliciosas
que yo he comido jamás.**

Your tortillas are the most delicious I have ever eaten.

An Encounter with Tech Support

The smooth jazz is pleasant,
despite repeated interruptions
assuring me that my call
is very important.

I start a mental shopping list,
but Myra breaks in between
bananas and dill pickles
to ask how she might help.
Myra sounds young.

I tell her that for mysterious reasons,
their Brother printer and my Mac
are no longer on speaking terms.

Myra offers her condolences,
then guides me through
a maze of printer screens,
more than the universe
should be able to hold.
Scroll up, press okay,
scroll down, press okay,
Myra says over and over.

I offer my own condolences
as Myra waits in silence
for me to scroll and press
through the alphabet,
A to T, and back to b,
lower case, upper case,
back to lower case.
Like texting with a flip phone.
It's a very long password,

I say, then ask her if she is longing
for fresh paint to watch dry right now.

Being monitored for quality assurance
must dull your sense of humor,
for Myra does not laugh.

Myra, I wonder, did you imagine
this future as you walked
across the stage to receive handshake
and sheepskin and toss your tassel?

I imagine her as a brunette. I bet she's
very nice once she warms up to you.

At last Brother printer and Mac
have reconciled. I tell Myra
I hope she sometimes deals with
more interesting problems than mine.
There is hesitation, then hint of a sigh.
You don't know the half of it, she says.
I urge her to have a nice day.

O child of God   child of Allah   child of war

you'd think the inner dome of heaven had fallen,*
its deadly stars raining on this struggling land.

Shards of whistling light

streak the midnight sky

so lovely in flight

so heedless of

our prayers.

Do not try to catch the stars
my precious one,
but quickly hide
hide in your mother's arms
close your eyes
cover your ears.
Pray to God   to Allah
that for this shower
of stars   you are not
its mark.

And if at dawn you still have eyes
and ears, go outside to see how the stars
have reordered your universe.
Pick up a chunk of what was once
your roof   a neighbor's home,
consider its many uses
and if you are resilient
if you can still heed the mandate
of childhood to find light
in the darkest place
and create a moment free of fear

I pray, little one,
that you can use it
for play.

* *you'd think the inner dome of heaven had fallen* is taken from *Birches,* by Robert Frost.

When my mother died

I did not cry.
I watched dry-eyed

as the gray plastic shroud
was taken from our home.

By the time the hospital bed
and commode were gone

I'd begun to turn her dying
room back into a dining room.

I bristled when strangers said
What a blessing to live to 100!

This woman who taught me to recite
Little Orphant Annie at seven

who sang of picking pansies in spring
who said once that a glass of ice water

gave any dinner table a little swank
and gave our family a running joke

this woman who Dad said
was friendly as a wet cocker spaniel

who never got over her crush
on Adlai Stevenson

who couldn't understand
why no one in her assisted living

was concerned about the war in Syria
became herself like a refugee

struggling to build a warm fire
in the rubble of a bombed out building.

Joy she gave, joy she has found
was what she wanted on her tombstone.

She tried lord she tried so hard to find the joy
that once flowed through her like an easy river
until at last her joy-making machinery
broke down and could not be repaired.

Why am I still here? she asked me
over and over. I had no answer except

to be an example to others
of dying with grace.

My wisdom was of no use to her.
Only being of use made sense.

In the end she went for days
without food or water.

Who knew a century-old body
could survive on air?

Her last words to me –
This is disgusting.

So no, when my mother died I did not cry.
Not then.

Early Evening in the Grand Canyon

I am drunk on sky and rock
in the golden hour when sun
bathes ageless canyon walls
carves slanted shadows

I am drunk on clouds
hugging the horizon like
mounds of silver-laced snow

I am drunk on the sweep
of open space of time
beneath me
where layers of sage
sienna
copper
henna
angle their way
to the ribbon of river far below
which runs from eternity to eternity
without thought

I am now nothing more than eyes and mind
as this weary body tethered
to past and future
melds into the rock that gives me rest
into the sand under my feet
into timeless sky
into the ineffable rightness
of everything flooding my spirit

Getting a Buzz on at Cliff Bell's

A second glass of wine
smooths the rough edges of the world.
Through a haze of Chardonnay,
my husband is more handsome,
my friends so clever, so dear.

Did the server describe this wine
as oaky or buttery? No matter,
he clearly knew just what
would enhance the Art Moderne
vibe of this club.

Is that Joan Crawford with
Clark Gable in a far corner?
The resemblance is uncanny,
but my focus is soft, like the lens
used on post-ingenue Doris Day.

The man on stage in sharkskin
suit and porkpie hat croons
of love fulfilled,
the one who done him wrong,
steamy sex.

I close my eyes and wish
for a world always as lovely
as the one I see tonight
through Chardonnay.

My Life as a Tree

1.
Once upon a time I hiked into a fairy tale

set in the Hoh Rainforest
where I'd never been in human form.
But that day decades ago

ancient relatives enfolded me
into the towering western hemlock
they told me I'd once been.

Sitka spruce and I caught up
on centuries of gossip
whispered in the breeze.

Old man's beard and witches' hair
hung like curtains
over my limbs

and chanterelle mushrooms
jostled ferns for room
among my roots.

Around my gnarly feet
a deep bed of moss
invited weary hikers to rest.

English ivy snaked around my trunk
and peregrine falcon
fleetest of hunters

sailed above the dense overstory
its lethal eye on a hapless
mourning dove.

I believe I even heard for a moment
the steady tap-tap of a leprechaun's
hammer crafting tiny shoes.

But I could not remain a hemlock
for I wanted to move about
and liked having opposable thumbs

so I walked from the forest
my heavy boots on pine needles
leaving no trace of our family reunion.

2.
There is much to be said
for having once been a tree.

When a thought flits into my brain
then flies away too soon

I tell myself the thought was simply
the ghost of a rainforest sparrow

ever busy
ever moving

reminding me that I was once its home.

My beloved world

is red & hot as a steel factory furnace
      & cool aquamarine swimming pool green

My beloved world tastes like burnt toast
      under a silky slathering of honey

smells like sulfur & soot
      & the soft spot on a newborn's head

feels like a bed of nails
      buried under pillows of cotton candy

My beloved world is loud as the screams of war
      & the joyful celebration of a soldier's return

I don't wish to stay until midnight
    in this clamorous world
        & I want to embrace its beauty
          & stay to see
            what happens on the day after
            the day after

Ineffable as Blood

When I consider the River Jordan carrying life
to the distant regions of my body, consider
the twelve keepers of that river —

fibrinogen, prothrombin, thromboplastin and such —
as they perform their delicate dance – gliding
in perfect time to keep the river flowing,

when I consider that if one dancer trips,
misses a step, the river of blood floods its banks
or forms a deadly logjam,

I can only wonder what choreographed this
dance, eons in the making, a mystery to mortal
minds? Evolution of course — the right answer,

but one so lacking in awe. With no wish to argue
the existence or nature of god, I think perhaps now
and then I should take a moment to give thanks,

knowing this miraculous river
is all I need of the sacred.

To My Neighbor, Old Cottonwood

Why didn't you tell us you were
unwell, your weary roots rotting?

How well you hid
the subterranean wreckage
the way one might mask the signs
of a troubled marriage, until
the moment a fierce gust of wind
shoved you across the neighbor's
back porch and onto our roof,
where you rested over our house
like the vines covering
Sleeping Beauty's castle.

Thank you, Old Cottonwood,
for aiming your deadly arc away
from our screened-in back porch,
where I stood
under an aluminum roof
closing windows
to protect us from
the coming storm.

Exhortation to Self, on Turning 75

This is not your first Rubicon.
Pray it won't be your last.
Give thanks to the god of serendipity.
You are among the lucky ones.

At 60 you thought you were
only a few aerobics classes
away from a rerun of 45.
You were not.
At 75 you'll never see 60 again.
Get over it.

Mount your bike with step-through
so low you could nap on it.
One foot on the pedal, the other
pushing once twice three times
if needed to get aloft.
No one's counting.

Feel the sudden breeze,
the moment of weightlessness
that assures you this was
a good idea. Dial the gear
up to six though you hate six.

Take pride in your choice of color.
Construction cone orange
makes kids call out *Nice bike!*
as you roll by.

Ignore the young woman
with long muscular strides
swallowing the sidewalk,
blond ponytail in flight.
You are not her and never were.

Ride with a plan or no plan.
But ride.

www.ingramcontent.com/pod-product-compliance
Lightning Source LLC
Chambersburg PA
CBHW061708120626
46550CB00003B/1149